"Roger Rosenblatt is one of our most gifted essayists—wise, funny, and insightful. I will happily carry his *Rules for Aging* into my sunset years and trust them to chart my course to geezerhood." —TOM BROKAW

"I plan to reshape my life so that I may live by [*Rules for Aging*]. I only wish I could start all over again so I could, like Mr. Rosenblatt, attain perfection. My favorites are rules 1, 15, 18, 24, 41, and 49." —JIM LEHRER

"I like this book and am thinking it over. Especially rules 1, 3, 16—wish I'd known that about 15 years ago—and 38, and 57. And 34—'It's not about you'—that's worth the price of the book." —GARRISON KEILLOR

"In this charming, often insightful little book, [Rosenblatt] goes for laughs, but there's always a grain of truth there. . . . We may not achieve perfection with *Rules for Aging* but we probably will live longer, happier lives."
—*THE TIMES-PICAYUNE* (NEW ORLEANS)

"Easy, enjoyable reading, and there's nothing quite like that warm feeling you get from having your finest qualities reaffirmed by an expert."
—*MINNEAPOLIS STAR TRIBUNE*

"An entertaining little journey . . . [Rosenblatt] seems to have modeled [*Rules for Aging*] after the *Don't Sweat the Small Stuff* books, except that Rosenblatt is more succinct."
—*HOUSTON CHRONICLE*

"Rosenblatt lays out a road map for aging with grace. . . . All told, Rosenblatt offers 58 witty rules for getting along by going along."
—*RICHMOND TIMES-DISPATCH*

"With its mix of bite-size aphorisms and literary erudition, Rosenblatt's primer reads like a charming cross between Ambrose Bierce and Michel de Montaigne. . . . Rosenblatt's fortune-cookie pronouncements offer light diversion for those final moments before a bedside reader shuts out the light." —*THE ADVOCATE* (BATON ROUGE)

"*Rules for Aging* is a front-of-the-counter book. . . . It's a handy little impulse buy of the kind beloved by publishers; fun to read, soon forgotten, but nonetheless full of caustic wisdom." —*THE EAST HAMPTON STAR*

"A hilarious guide to life . . . Delightfully smart and to the point." —*PEOPLE*

RULES FOR
AGING

RULES FOR
AGING

A Wry and Witty
Guide to Life

ROGER ROSENBLATT

A HARVEST BOOK
HARCOURT, INC.
San Diego   New York   London

www.HarcourtBooks.com

Library of Congress Cataloging-in-Publication Data
Rosenblatt, Roger.
Rules for aging: resist normal impulses, live longer, attain
perfection/Roger Rosenblatt.
p. cm.
ISBN 0-15-100659-8
ISBN 0-15-601360-6 (pbk.)
1. Aging—Humor.   2. Conduct of life—Humor.   3. Aging.
4. Conduct of life.   I. Title.
PN6231.A43 R67 2000
818'.5402—dc21   00-033539

Text set in ITC Caslon 224
Designed by Lois Stanfield, LightSource Images

Printed in the United States of America

First Harvest edition 2001
A C E G I K J H F D B

For Ginny
(see 21a.)

Introduction

This little guide is intended for people who wish to age successfully, or at all. I very much hope that older readers may profit from it as much as younger ones, but the fact that one has achieved at least middle age suggests that one has already heeded most of the rules provided here. One may think of this work as a how-to book, akin to the many health guides published these days, whose purpose is to prolong our lives and make them richer. That is the aim of my book, too. Growing older is as much an art as it is a science, and it requires fewer things to do than not to do.

What follows, then, is mainly a list of "don't"s and "not"s, not unlike the Ten Commandments, but without the moral base. The rules herein are intended to be purely practical. When I urge you to refrain from a certain thought or course of action, I do not mean to suggest that you are in any way wrong if you do the opposite. I mean only to say that you will suffer.

The rules are numbered consecutively for your convenience. Once you commit them all to memory, you may find it easier to simply refer to the appropriate number. Otherwise nothing is required of the reader but a willingness to change one's entire way of looking at things. Resist every normal impulse, and a perfect life is yours forever. Good luck.

Roger Rosenblatt

The Rules

A READY REFERENCE TABLE

RULES FOR
AGING

1

It doesn't matter

Whatever you think matters—doesn't. Follow this rule, and it will add decades to your life. It does not matter if you are late, or early; if you are here, or if you are there; if you said it, or did not say it; if you were clever, or if you were stupid; if you are having a bad hair day, or a no hair day; if your boss looks at you cockeyed; if your girlfriend or boyfriend looks at you cockeyed; if you are cockeyed; if you don't get that promotion, or prize, or house, or if you do. It doesn't matter.

2

Nobody is
thinking about you

$\sim\!\!\!\!\sim$

Yes, I know, you are certain that your friends are becoming your enemies; that your grocer, garbageman, clergyman, sister-in-law, and your dog are all of the opinion that you have put on weight, that you have lost your touch, that you have lost your mind; furthermore, you are convinced that everyone spends two-thirds of every day commenting on your disintegration, denigrating your work, plotting your assassination. I promise you: Nobody is thinking about you. They are thinking about themselves—just like you.

3

Let bad enough alone

This rule requires some amplification because it involves one of the more complicated, charming, and lethal human faculties—optimism—specifically the optimism that embraces the belief that persistent clarification after one has committed a social blunder will make everything all right.

On the afternoon of September 24, 1980, William Agee, chairman of the Bendix Corporation, experienced a fit of candor and decided to make a speech before 600 employees. His intention was to put at rest, once and for all, the rumors that his admittedly "close friendship" with attractive, blond 29-year-old Mary Cunningham had a connection with her professional rise from executive assistant to vice president for strategic planning in the stunningly short space of 15 months. Having thus cleared the air, Agee settled back to observe the story of his affair with Cunningham dominate the headlines for many weeks—in a news era that could otherwise have been interested in a war in the Middle East and a plunging stock market.

After Agee's clarifying exercise, his company issued a statement that a "major disclosure" would be forthcoming; but upon further reflection, Agee decided that "we just didn't have any more to say." Too bad that came a bit late. Soon he and Cunningham left Bendix in disgrace to become enshrined in American business folklore—not because they had sinned or because Cunningham had been improperly promoted, but simply because of Agee's boyishly optimistic gesture.

A realist will always let bad enough alone, but a romantic cannot stop himself from saying just one more thing that will clear up the mess. Poor Agee had no idea that by making a clean breast of things, which is supposed to be good for the soul, as well as part of the American way, he would be snatching disaster from the jaws of suspicion.

He should have looked more closely into history before he leaped. His suicidal forthrightness placed him squarely in a most distinguished company of reckless clarifiers, all of whom, at one crucial, wretched moment of their lives, were possessed by the demonic inspiration that if they could only explain themselves fully in the throes of scandal—let it all hang out, lay their cards on the table, spare no detail, be up-front, come clean, and so forth—the grateful, enlightened public would stand as one and shout, "I see! Thank you!" and all would be forgiven.

This is how George F. Baer achieved American duncehood during the Pennsylvania coal strike of 1902 when a resident of Wilkes-Barre wrote to Baer, the chief spokesman for the mine owners, to express anxiety over the ravages of the strike. Baer decided to explain himself. In a letter that was later widely circulated, especially among the United Mine Workers, he reassured his correspondent that some people were placed on earth to manage and others to serve, and that this was the divine order of things. Said Baer: "The rights and interests of the laboring man will be protected and cared for, not by the labor agitators, but by the Christian men to whom God in His infinite wisdom has given control of the property interests of the country." So that was that.

Then there is William Jennings Bryan who, having seen his fundamentalist creed vindicated during the

Scopes trial of 1925, still insisted on taking the stand to make his antievolution position crystal clear. He did, thus exposing himself to national (and historical) ridicule. And there is Oveta Culp Hobby who, as Secretary of Health, Education and Welfare in 1955, explained the shortage of the new Salk polio vaccine with these words: "No one could have foreseen its great acclaim." And there is always Richard Nixon, the apostle of perfect clarity, who at times seemed hell-bent on clarifying himself out of office.

As the wise have always told us, the lesson in all such instances is: remember the abiding value of keeping one's mouth shut. Not for nothing did La Rochefoucauld call silence "the best tactic for him who distrusts himself." It is not simply that silence is generally prudent; it also encourages the presumption of virtue, appearing— especially in times of adversity—as a sign of both discretion and suffering. But the best reasons for keeping one's counsel, especially during a scandal, have to do with common sense:

> a. Every time someone makes a public confession, his audience grows conscious of their own secret sins. The mere presence of the

confessor is mortifying and implicitly incriminating. The audience cannot take it. The more direct his approach, the more they want to get rid of him. Carnage ensues.

b. Nobody ever really wants a scandal cleared up. Uncleared-up, a scandal is like radio—it allows the imagination to rove like a child in a flower field, especially when an office romance is involved, and the imagination may cavort among infinite possibilities of after-hour adventures behind the desk—legs sprawling wildly among the Eberhard Fabers, Muzak stuck on *Boléro*. When the candid spoilsport steps forward to tell it like it actually was, the imagination's freedom is curtailed. The audience grows vengeful. Carnage ensues.

In the modern world, William Jefferson Clinton became a fine example of how letting bad enough alone can save one's neck. Much has been made of the fact that Clinton's unusual relationship with Monica Lewinsky almost cost him his job. But except for the delicate negotiations in White House hallways and a predisposition for distractions while making phone calls,

Clinton brilliantly handled his extraordinary mess by never saying any more about it than needed to be said. Indeed, if he had told reporters at the outset: "I never slept with that woman, Miss Lewinsky," rather than "I never had sexual relations with that woman," and then if he had added, "My private life belongs to me and my family, and I will not waste the nation's time by discussing it further," he might have been off the hook earlier. Yet, he still did the right thing by saying as little as possible, especially to reporters. Reporters want you to say as much as possible, which should tell you all you need to know.

4

Ignore your enemy
or kill him

～◯

In this world you have to be oh-so-smart
or oh-so-pleasant. For years I was smart.
I recommend pleasant.

—Harvey the Rabbit

S o do I, generally. There is a special context, though, in which one can be smart by being pleasant. It occurs in one of those very unpleasant situations in life when you recognize that you are faced with an enemy of a particular sort—someone to whom you have done no harm, yet who, nonetheless, seethes with a hissing fury at the mere mention of your name, yips like a terrier whenever you enjoy good fortune, and bites the newspaper when there is a report of your success. Now, here is one person who *is* thinking about you. In an odd way, he lives for you. Your every move gives definition to his existence.

Ayn Rand created such a character in her nutty novel, *The Fountainhead*, with the critic who relentlessly savages the work of Howard Roark the architect, no matter how demonstrably wonderful Roark's work is. Rand painted the critic as one who would have no reason for being if he could not attack Roark at every turn. In Roark's presence, he glowers at the architect like a hungry rat—eyes squinting and burning—knowing that he is too small to devour his quarry, yet desperate to do damage or, in the very least, to be noticed by Roark for the damage he attempts to inflict.

For his part, Roark ignores the man entirely. He goes about his work unconscious of this critic or of anybody who might interfere with his vision. His attitude has a kind of Nietzschean charm, but it protects him from bothersome disturbances. Finally, the critic cannot take being ignored any longer, so he confronts Roark with all the awful things he has written about the architect. He asks, half plaintively: "What do you think of me?" Roark, as if seeing the man for the first time, responds: "I don't think of you." The critic withers and slinks off.

It is Rand's version of the scene in *Casablanca* where Peter Lorre says to Bogart: "You despise me, don't you?" and Bogart replies: "I would if I bothered to think about you."

In the realm of normal human behavior (whatever that may be), it is probably impossible to be as oblivious as Roark is when there is someone around continually seeking to do you harm, indeed, whose bitter happiness seems to depend on it. Only a person with the hide of an elephant could really pay no attention when such an enemy is relentlessly firing insults and slinging mud. Who would not feel some slight hurt, if only because someone exists who is consumed with the desire to bring you low?

And yet, here—as in so many rules of aging—the trick is to do absolutely nothing. Nothing is everything. Ignore your enemy or kill him. If you pay no attention to him, he may not slink away, but he will grow increasingly desperate, increasingly incoherent, and (best of all) increasingly unhappy. The happier your life, the more miserable his. The truth is, that people of this peculiar stripe are their own worst enemy (admittedly, they have some heated competition), and it constitutes one of life's delights to watch them go at themselves with all the bitterness and disappointment of which they are composed. To enjoy this, however, one must never give them a scintilla of assistance.

Of course, as the complete rule suggests, one can take a different approach, and, instead of ignoring one's enemy, one can murder him. If he is really getting to you, I advise that you do it. But you must kill quickly, suddenly, and anonymously, or it's no good—with a bomb, perhaps, or a flamethrower shot from a great distance. You want him dead, but you do not want him to see that it was you doing him in. If he knows it is you, all is lost. In that billionth of a second, he will die content that he got your goat and that all his efforts have finally paid off—which is the last thing you want.

For myself, I favor giving one's enemy life without parole instead of an execution. Think of it, the beauty of it: You are his obsession, and he is merely a bark in the night. The idea is not to care, not to pretend that you don't care, but to really not care. Trust me. You have just extended your enviable life.

5

Boo yourself off the stage

∼⌒

C harles Lamb attended the opening of one of his plays and, having seen that the thing was very bad, stood up and started to boo—beating the rest of the audience by seconds. Unlikely as it sounds, there may be one or two occasions in your life when you do something not up to your usual high standard. When that occurs, lead the booing yourself. It is good for one's health, and it will deprive others of the satisfaction of your embarrassment.

6

Yes you did

⌒

If you have the slightest question as to whether or not you are responsible for a wrongdoing, you are. As soon as you think, "I really didn't do it"—you did. Come to this conclusion early, act to correct it, and live a lot longer. Come to it late, act to correct it, and live a little longer. Don't come to it at all, never act to correct it, and . . . how are you feeling?

7

After the age of 30, it is unseemly to blame one's parents for one's life

~

Make that 25.

8

If something is boring you, it is probably you

~~~~~

This rule was inspired by Dylan Thomas, who used to talk incessantly, especially when looped. He was on a walking tour of the Scottish Isles, where, it was reported, he had been talking for two days straight. Finally he stopped, looked around, and said, "Somebody's boring me. I think it's me!"

9

Stay clear of anyone—other than a clergyman—who refers to God more than once in an hour

~~~◦

O ne sees a growing number of professional moralists who appear on TV telling people what God
wants of them. If these folks are right about God, it is
splendid news, and one should follow them as if they
were Moses. If, however, they have misinterpreted God's
wishes—about political candidates, free expression,
human reproduction, and other issues on which He is
said to be communicating His opinions to a select few—
or if these professional moralists have mistaken God's
voice for, say, Elvis's, then paying attention to them

may only lead to divine trouble. Better to play it safe and avoid such people. The danger in hanging around them is that God may be tired of listening to them misrepresent Him and decide to revert to His old bad-tempered tricks with locusts and floods. Of course, this being the 21st century, He may have refined His arsenal so that He can pick off only the offenders and leave the rest of us unharmed. But I would not count on this. God is good, but He may not be that good.

10

Swine rules

a. *A swine is not a swan.* Over a lifetime, one will encounter several swine—true lowlifes—and one is sometimes tempted to treat them kindly under the theory that, if shown kindness, they will be less swinelike and, perhaps, even reform. (Much laughter here.) As in rule 3, this is the sort of optimism that ought to be criminalized. A swine is a swine is a swine. He was almost certainly fully formed as a swine by age three, and he is not going to grow virtuous simply because you are burdened with hope. To be sure, there may be one swine in a billion who is susceptible to improvement, but why take chances? Even if you are wrong in one or two cases, you will still live longer, which, I remind you, is your objective.

b. *A swine is known to be a swine.* You may feel that though you know a swine for what he is, others do not. You may think, therefore, that when the swine does you dirt behind your back, others will accept his swinish opinion. Fear not. Everyone knows a swine to be a swine. He did not become famous by behaving swinishly toward you alone. You may turn your back with impunity.

c. *When a swine sucks up.* He is still a swine.

d. *A swine is a swine all the time.* While one might remember that a swine is not a swan, one is bound to forget that a swine is a swine all the time—either because he is not behaving swinishly toward you personally or because he appears to be in some temporarily unswinely state and bears all the outward signs of a decent human being. You know perfectly well that the swine is a swine. But he looks okay at the moment, so you let down your intelligence. You are so gulled that you might even do him a favor.

When you are tempted in this way, please recall the following joke my grandmother told me which, while not specifically about swine, does pertain to the laws of human consistency. A man on a visit to a lunatic asylum is suddenly approached by an inmate. The inmate calmly and politely asks the visitor if he may have a moment of his time. He explains carefully and in exquisitely rational detail why his incarceration in the asylum is a bureaucratic error, that someone has made a terrible mistake, and that he—who is perfectly sane—has been wrongly condemned for 10 years. The visitor, who first wishes to free himself of the inmate, begins to listen sympathetically. And eventually he determines that the man is indeed sane and sound and a victim of somebody's error.

"I will come back next Tuesday with the necessary papers for your release," he tells the inmate.

"Excellent," says the man, who then accompanies the visitor to the doorway, kicks him down the stairs, and calls out, "Don't forget next Tuesday."

11

Listen for the word "Great"

~~~~

I t is my experience that whenever anyone says the word "Great!" in response to an idea you have, or to some work you have accomplished, or to a proposal you have made, it is time to pack your bags. I don't know how this happened, but somewhere in the annals of insincerity, someone hit on this ingenious word, which is used to mislead others, to keep them at bay, or to relay no meaning whatever. The cleverness of the response is that it says the exact opposite of what it means. The one who uses the word could not be less thrilled about you or your idea. Yet nothing overtly discouraging has been said. Indeed, the word is often accompanied by an enthusiastic punch in the air, as if to indicate that you have just invented penicillin. In any case, pay no attention to it, or you'll be wasting more time. Act as if the person who said "Great!" has said "Interesting!" and go home.

12

Listen for the question "What are you talking about?"

S hould that question arise in response to an accu-sation, know for certain that the person who said it knows perfectly well what you are talking about. Respond accordingly.

13

Appearance is frequently reality

~

No matter what they told you in college.

14

Be not witty;
neither shalt thou be clever

~~~~~⁓

Wit and cleverness are odd forms of intelligence, if, in fact, they are forms of intelligence at all. I have known several dopes who are quite witty and many brilliant people who have never said a clever thing in their lives. Whenever I have resorted to wit myself, it is usually in a situation where I do not have a decent thought in my head and some pun or clever turn of phrase has jumped in as a last-minute understudy. Nonetheless, some clever or witty remarks occur to everyone, often with such delightful surprise that one cannot resist blurting them out for the benefit of others.

Resist, I beg of you. Resist especially at social gatherings, such as group lunches or dinner parties. If your remarks are truly witty, you may be certain that everyone will laugh, nod energetically in that knowing, intellectually appreciative way, and all the while regard you with an inward fear that will, one fine day, work to your disadvantage.

There have been, as far as I can count, four witty people in history. They are Oscar Wilde, Dorothy Parker, Winston Churchill, and Oscar Levant. One might add Mark Twain and James Whistler, but Whistler's wit seems mainly to have been used for boasting and Twain's usually evidenced itself in a broad, generous context. Generally, wit is neither broad nor generous, and history's four leading wits are principally known for putdowns. Their witty remarks have been quoted over and over by those who wish to get laughs in public, by anthologists, and by essayists in need of examples more clever than anything they themselves could produce. For example:

Oscar Levant, when asked by a draft board examiner, "Do you think you can kill?" replied: "I don't know about strangers, but friends, yes."

Dorothy Parker, when told that a London actress whom she disliked had broken her leg said: "How terrible! She must have done it sliding down a barrister."

A poet, who had been passed over for the Poet Laureateship of England, complained to Oscar Wilde: "It's a conspiracy of silence against me. What ought I to do, Oscar?" Wilde advised: "Join it."

Winston Churchill called Clement Attlee "a sheep in sheep's clothing," when he was not calling him "a modest little man with much to be modest about." Then there was this famous exchange:

Lady Astor: "Winston, if you were my husband, I should flavor your coffee with poison."

Churchill: "Madam, if I were your husband, I should drink it."

The fact that one has heard these remarks hundreds of times, along with a dozen well-known others, and that the group who made them can be tallied on less than one hand should tell us something about wit—and that something is not that wit is a rare and precious gift. What it tells us is that wit is a trick, something in the category of sawing a lady in half. It is briefly entertaining, and it belies something dangerous. People like it, but they are also afraid of it, and, given the opportunity, they will punish you for it.

Of the gang of four, Oscar Wilde should probably be awarded the cake. His creative life, which was considerable, virtually came to an end when he was shipped off to Reading Gaol for homosexual acts with Lord Alfred Douglas. In a gesture of grandiose stupidity, Wilde brought a criminal libel suit against Douglas's father, the Marquess of Queensbury, who had made the initial accusation against him. Wilde decided that it would be a good idea to clear his name and, thus, went to jail (see rule 3). He was characteristically witty throughout the trial, news of which was lavishly detailed in every newspaper in England. At one point, he told a friend who was embarrassed to mention the trial in conversation: "You've heard of my case. Don't distress yourself. All is well. The working classes are with me . . . to a boy."

That kind of cleverness undoubtedly led to Wilde's spending two years at hard labor—that, of course, and the brainstorm of bringing the suit in the first place. It must be said in fairness, as well as in admiration, that Wilde had a soul as great as his wit. Standing in pouring rain, while waiting to be transported to the jail, he remarked: "If this is the way Queen Victoria treats her prisoners, she doesn't deserve to have any."

But the general trouble with wit is that it is almost always used for slinging insults. If one hears a witty insult, no matter how verbally stunning, one knows in one's heart that the same little genius who delivered it is capable of being just as witty about you, and in the throes of your laughter, you dislike that person, at least at that moment. Wit is comedy, not humor. Comedy cuts life off; humor enlarges and embraces it. People known for wit are invariably also known for a certain coldness and for keeping other people at a distance. Make a note of those you know who tell lots of jokes in social gatherings and tell me if you like them.

15

Pursue virtue,
but don't sweat it

What you mean "we"?
—attributed to Tonto

Pepys the diarist was known to commit every sin within his reach, yet Dr. Johnson called him a virtuous man because he knew the difference between good and bad behavior and strove for the former, though the latter came easier. It is a useful definition of virtue—this knowing the difference—because it is as close to purely virtuous behavior as we animals are likely to get. Aging involves the cyclical repetition of so many wrongdoings (Will I ever learn? No.) that continued self-flagellation can grow quite depressing. But if one strives for a sort of enlightened imperfection and stops beating oneself over the head for every transgression, life can seem almost tolerable.

As an example I offer the virtue of loyalty, which is always raised aloft as a standard for noble action, but which, as far as I can tell, is never achieved.

Sooner or later, in big things or small, everybody betrays everybody—not necessarily out of malice, but because loyalty runs counter to our makeup. "Into what danger would you lead me, Cassius?" asks Brutus, who is, in fact, an honorable man, yet he is easily seduced to treason by an envious one. I can still hear George McGovern's avowal of fealty to his running mate, Thomas Eagleton, in the 1972 presidential campaign, after it was revealed that Eagleton had undergone electroshock therapy. "I'm behind him one thousand percent," said McGovern, shortly before dumping him.

I have always suspected that a bank with "Fidelity" in its title is going to lose my money. The mere assertion of loyalty is often enough to signal betrayal. One of the weaknesses of loyalty is that, unlike friendship, it requires some outward demonstration or declaration and so invites insincerity. Loyalty is also, by implication, unconditional and suggests that although you do not agree with the person or institution to which you are expected to stick, you will do so anyway. All this practically guarantees treason.

How to spot someone who is likely to be disloyal: 1) Anyone who feels underappreciated and makes a lot of noise about it. If he'd flattered Cassius once in a while, Caesar would be alive today. 2) Anyone who feels inadequate in his or her position, high or low, and fears exposure. 3) Anyone who writes a newspaper column. 4) Anyone who wants to. 5) Anyone who spends a good deal of time reading travel brochures or in a Mercedes showroom. 6) Anyone whose name contains a vowel. 7) Anyone else.

As noble a standard as loyalty sets, there is simply too much fear, self-doubt, opportunism, ambition, and, occasionally, principled thinking in the human mind to expect people to adhere to it. So unachievable is this goal that it is usually the betrayals that make life interesting. (See John Dean and Nixon; David Stockman and Reagan; Judas and Jesus.) To be sure, there are people famous for loyalty, but they are often loyal to a fault, and a supposed virtue becomes pathetic, stupid, and sometimes criminal. Rose Mary Woods entered history when she stood by her man's tape recorder. Hubert Humphrey probably lost the presidency when he stuck by Lyndon

Johnson and his Vietnam policies; a sign of character was regarded as a flaw. Then there was Mrs. Odysseus.

Of course, the worst manifestations occur when institutions or governments mandate loyalty with phrases like "the national interest" (Kennedy kept journalists silent with that trick) or with loyalty oaths. During the McCarthy shame, graduate students were required to sign loyalty oaths when they applied for government grants. A dean at Harvard defended this practice as being merely pro forma—of no greater significance than licking the stamps for the application envelopes. At a faculty meeting, the great Italian scholar Renato Paggioli stood up and commented: "Mr. Dean, I am from fascist Italy, and I will tell you something. First you licka the stamps, then you licka something else."

To return to the rule: Pursue virtue, but don't sweat it. The pursuit alone is sufficient to establish your qualities, and if you fail once in a while, your guilt will remind you of the right path you didn't take. Auden had it right in the poem "Lullaby" that begins: "Lay your sleeping head, my love, / Human on my faithless arm." Ah, humans.

16

Do not go to your left

~~~

G oing to one's left—or working on going to one's
left—is a basketball term for strengthening
one's weakness. A right-handed player will improve his
game considerably if he learns to dribble and shoot with
his left hand and to move to his left on the court. What
is true for basketball, however, is not true for living.
In life, if you attempt to compensate for a weakness,
you will usually grow weaker. If, on the other hand (the
right one), you keep playing to your strength, people
will not notice that you have weaknesses. Of course, you
probably do not believe this. You will want to take sing-
ing lessons anyway.

One reason this rule is so hard to obey, apart from
one's personal inclinations, is that there is a great deal
of nonsensical social pressure on someone who does

one thing very well—and who is acknowledged for doing that thing very well—to change direction and do something else—usually very poorly. The comic actor Bill Murray is a case in point. When Murray is at the top of his game, which is nearly all the time, there is no funnier actor in America. He uses exaggerated seriousness expertly; he never overplays or overstates; and he has perfected the lunatic confidence of the total incompetent who is, at the same time, romantically appealing.

Because all this is so, and because Murray is demonstrably wonderful as a comic actor, critics are continually urging him to succeed in "serious," "deep," and "moving" roles, instead of rewarding him for having played to his strength. Murray, because he is driven by some out-of-whack interior compass and because the critics eat up his mistakes, continues to take on such ill-fitting roles as the rich businessman in *Rushmore* and the unintentionally hilarious artist in Somerset Maugham's infinitely morose *The Razor's Edge*. He thinks he is compensating, but he is merely wasting time.

Or take Michael Jordan. In his case, there was no critical prompting behind his decision to take a year off from the Chicago Bulls to play baseball for the Chicago White Sox; it was all his own idea. And if that useless year turned out to be fun for Jordan, more power to him. Indeed, as a New York Knicks fan, I would have been delighted to see him take off one more year for golf, another for tennis, another for botany—anything to keep him away from Madison Square Garden. But in truth, baseball was a waste of time for the greatest basketball player ever. He should have stayed on the court.

Murray tries to be what he is not and Jordan does the same because we punish ourselves with the cultural expectation that the highest achievement in life is to be a "renaissance man" (or woman). The oddity of this designation is that there were precious few people in any renaissance (Italian, English, or Irish) who could do more than one thing well. (Pace, Michelangelo.) What they did well, they did surpassingly well. I don't recall Dante creating anything that held a candle to the *Divine Comedy*. Shakespeare, Marlowe, and Kyd could write plays *and* poems, but in those days they were much the same thing. Yeats couldn't write great plays any more than Synge could write great poems. None of these renaissance men gave a moment's thought to his left.

Establish your strength and strengthen it. English critic Hilaire Belloc advised that a young and aspiring writer "concentrate on one subject. Let him, when he is

20, write about the earthworm. Let him continue for 40 years to write of nothing but the earthworm. When he is 60, pilgrims will make a hollow path with their feet to the door of the world's great authority on the earthworm. They will knock at his door and humbly beg to be allowed to see the Master of the Earthworm."

To be sure, Belloc was specifically addressing the writer "who is merely thinking of fame." But what writer is not? Find thy earthworm.

17

Everyone's work is magnificent

~~~~~

This rule applies to those occasions when people, often total strangers, have decided that you are the one person on earth to assess the merits of their oil painting, cooking, wood carving, sand sculpture, dress design, electric train setup, love song, or the 30,000-line tragicomic epic poem they have composed on the life of John Gotti, which they have never shown to anyone until today. They "know what an imposition" their request is. But they seek your "frank opinion" because they "really respect your judgment." Here is your judgment: "It's magnificent." Do not add a syllable. Shake their hand warmly, slap them on the back heartily, grin, and get out of there. If you believe that they wanted to hear anything other than "magnificent," you need a lot more help than they do.

18

Consult everyone on everything and don't forget to send ingratiating notes

❧

Here, I confess, is a rule I have never followed, and I have undoubtedly paid dearly for my neglect. It is based on the sad fact that no one in the world except your family and closest friends wants you to succeed, and so, whenever you do, people are prepared to express, or act upon, their resentment.

They will do so only if you haven't consulted them at every stage of your ascent. Conversely, if you select the most potentially dangerous of your "friends" and colleagues, take them aside in a series of melodramatically clandestine conferences, and ask them any number of insincere and purposeless questions regarding your future, the danger will dissipate, and they are likely to be on your side forever, or at least until good fortune comes your way again.

Among the confidential "please don't tell anyone" questions you might ask are "Do you think I ought to take the job?"; "What do you think is the main thing one ought to do in this position?"; "Is this job really doable, or am I headed for disaster?"; "What kind of help will I need?" This last question is especially useful because it strongly suggests that if you take the job (which you surely have already taken), you will engage the person you are confiding in as your close adviser, perhaps second-in-command. Once brought into your confidence, these people will feel a partnership in your rise and will be flattered that you have asked their advice. They will leave you alone, even support you against people like themselves.

You may reasonably ask: Why should I consult anybody, when I don't really need anyone's advice? Won't they see through this ploy and, instead of being flattered, feel insulted, even manipulated? No, they will not. Even if they do see through you, they will persuade themselves that they are being overly suspicious because, now that they think of it, they are worthy of your trust. It is a simple biological fact that no one is ever insulted by being consulted by a successful person.

You may reasonably ask: How long does this fakery go on? How long do I have to keep up these meaningless consultations? The answer is: Forever. Once you have achieved your high position without a scratch, it is extremely important that you continue your confidential consultations. Think of them as oil changes. I know how tiresome and tedious this sounds, but I have seen too many incidents where perfectly able people have suffered immeasurably from sensible and honest behavior.

Now to the ingratiating notes. When you think you have debased yourself below anything you might have imagined, take one step lower. Send the person you have consulted a thank-you note. Please do not ask why you should express gratitude for a response to a question you never meant to ask or needed to have answered in the first place. Just do it. In fact, it is a good subrule to send as many fawning notes to as many people as possible—all the time. I know two or three people who have virtually created careers by sending notes to those who might help (or injure) them. These notes need say nothing more than: "Loved your column"; "Loved your memo"; "Loved your comma." Yet they are as effective for self-protection and self-promotion as the work of ten public relations firms.

This said, I return to the confession that I have rarely, if ever, followed my own advice. But I have also failed in most of the few high positions I have held. Look upon me as a negative example. If you are interested in climbing upward, consult endlessly, and endlessly write notes. Of course, if you are not, forget this rule and sleep through the night.

19

Strife is better than loneliness

~~~~~~~

This is an old Irish proverb that I have stolen for one of my rules. I do not trust in it as wholeheartedly as I do the others because one can find oneself in situations so bellicose and stressful that a state of loneliness—indeed, of solitary confinement—may begin to look attractive. In balance, though, a combative existence is preferable, but it is probably wiser to avoid both extremes. To put it another way, see rule 21.

20

And loneliness is better than Eggs Benedict

～～

Whenever one is beginning to feel isolated from one's fellows, a countervailing impulse usually takes hold that suggests life will be greatly improved if one phones a lot of semi-friends and makes several dates for brunch—or otherwise seeks the company of people without the sight of whom one could live happily forever. Once these plans are made ("Brunch! At noon! What fun!"), one immediately realizes that the proposed event will be a predictable horror, and its various depressing moments will be experienced even before it has occurred. ("Eggs Benedict! I can't remember when I last had Eggs Benedict!")

Much sorrow may be avoided by acknowledging that as gloomy as being alone makes you feel, it is rollicking heaven compared with being among most other people. ("Belgian waffles! Do you really think they come from Belgium? Ha ha ha!")

21

Male and female compatibility rules

a. She's right.

b. He's really thinking about nothing. Really.

22

Run when you hear any of the following in a sentence

⌒⌒

". . . unity and harmony."

". . . love, unity, and harmony."

". . . humanity."

". . . the human condition."

". . . the human spirit."

23

Never miss an opportunity
to do nothing

~⌒○

No grand meaningless gesture. No unnecessary phone call. No gratuitous compliment. No retaliatory act. No desperate lurching for the approval of others. No . . . do I really have to go on?

24

Do not go for Cyrano's nose

A particularly satisfying scene in *Cyrano de Bergerac* occurs when a lout seeks to attack the hero by making fun of his monumental nose. Cyrano waits patiently as the lout delivers some obvious and pathetic insults. Then, instead of running him through with his sword—which he is quite capable of doing—he steps forward to present his own list of insults to his nose, all of which are brilliant and funny; and while they appear to be self-deprecating, they actually constitute a devastating mockery of the lout's intelligence—an attack far more effective than anything the lout ever could have devised.

Apart from innate stupidity, the lout's error lay in making his attack personal. People do this all the time—on figures public and private—because it is the first and easiest mode of attack that comes to mind. It transports one back to the school yard, where everyone one disliked was a "fatty" or a "dummy." Yet it does no more long-lasting damage than an invective shouted by a drunk from a moving car. I take that back—the damage it does is wholly to the drunk.

If one really wants to bring someone low, attack his or her ideas or opinions and not the person. Do it coldly and without a hem of passion showing. Also, be honest with one's criticism; do not distort the attackee's meaning by elliptical quotations or by false selection. Be occasionally magnanimous as well, even if disingenuously. One must remember that in an attack, the attacker is no less on display than the attackee. The result one seeks is to have people conclude that a scoundrel has been assaulted by a nobleman, not the reverse.

The one group I know of that has never learned this rule of sticking to the matter and not the person is writers. And, in this regard, they offer a useful example of how not to attack—and how not to live. As I write this entry, in fact, a typical and typically pointless literary battle is underway. John Irving has just attacked Tom Wolfe as being unreadable. Wolfe responded by attacking Irving as being washed-up as a novelist, along with Norman Mailer and John Updike, who had attacked Wolfe earlier. So it has always gone. Truman Capote on Jack Kerouac: "That's not writing, it's typing." Gore Vidal on Capote: "He has made lying an art. A minor art." The novelist James Gould Cozzens, perhaps expressing sour grapes of wrath: "I cannot read 10 pages of Steinbeck without throwing up."

Jazz musicians say only the most adoring things about one another; actors, generally the same. Only writers claw and spit, even though nobody cares but other writers, and public opinion of the attackee is affected not at all.

Yet here is H. L. Mencken's generous assessment of Henry James: "An idiot and a Boston idiot to boot, than which there is nothing lower in this world." And William Allen White's gracious description of Mencken: "With a pig's eye that never looks up, with a pig's snout that loves muck, with a pig's brain that knows only the sty, and a pig's squeal that cries only when he is hurt, he sometimes opens his pig's mouth, tusked and ugly, and lets out the voice of God, railing at the whitewash that covers the manure about his habitat." Small attack big; big attack small.

One trouble with the genre of insult is that it makes for wasteful digressions in a writer's career and is the antithesis of real, worthy writing itself. The aim of real writing is to make lives larger, more alert, and, with luck, happier. Attack writing is personal and seeks to do personal injury; it shrivels up everything it touches, by going for the nose.

It is also, by nature and intention, unfair and incomplete and frequently irrational. Macaulay said of Socrates, "The more I read him, the less I wonder that they poisoned him"—which might have made sense if Socrates (whom we know only from Plato) had left anything to read. Charles Kingsley called Shelley "a lewd vegetarian"—an intriguing idea but difficult to picture.

And it creates a false sense of accomplishment. Friends of an attacker will always rush to congratulate him on the meanness of his attack, because they get a two-fer: One writer has been belittled, and another has looked like a jackass doing it.

All enmity is personal, but it must not be made to sound that way. During a performance of Sheridan's *The Rivals*, the actor playing Sir Lucius O'Trigger was suddenly hit by an apple thrown by someone in the audience. "By the powers," he exclaimed. "Is it me, or the matter?" Always make it the matter.

25

That couldn't be a book

~~~

From time to time people will respond to an idea of yours, or to something you casually say, with the encouraging words "That could be a book!" It couldn't. It's not that the encouragers do not mean what they are saying; it's simply that they do not know what a book entails. Books are made out of big ideas, big themes, big actions, and big people, or at least they ought to be.

Take *Rules for Aging*, for instance. A very good-looking fellow comes out with one or two mildly amusing quips. Someone says: "That could be a book!" See what I mean?

26

Do not keep company with
people who speak of careers

⌒

Not only are such people uninteresting in themselves; they also have no interest in anything
interesting. They often form cliques, putatively for
social pleasure, actually for self-advancement and self-
protection. Sometimes these tight little gatherings have
the semblance of shared affection, but they are based on
the idea that each of its members is valuable according
to what he or she has achieved, is achieving, and what
he or she can do for the other members.

Keep company with people who are interested in
the world outside themselves. The one who never asks
you what you are working on; who never inquires as to
the success of your latest project; who never uses the
word career as a noun—he is your friend.

27

Just because the person who criticizes you is an idiot doesn't make him wrong

⌒

You would like to think his idiocy makes him wrong, but it doesn't. Treat all criticism as if it has been produced by the monkey with the typewriter; that is, see it as a lucky shot that happened to hit the mark. That way, you can make corrective use of the assault, yet denigrate the source. You still have your pride, after all.

28

Never go to a cocktail party, and, in any case, do not stay more than 20 minutes

꧁

I am an especially inept social creature who inevitably either says too much or too little at the very few cocktail parties to which I am invited and who inevitably leaves in a state of despondency that could require medication. If you are endowed with gregariousness, pay no attention to at least the first part of this rule. But if you share my ineptitude and find that you must attend a party, do the following:

Arrive at the exact hour that the party was announced to begin. No one arrives at that time; you will be able to make a beeline for the hosts so that they will definitely know that you were there. To be doubly sure of this, shake their hands vigorously. Show excessive good humor. Wear loud clothing.

Having smiled and nodded a lot and said many hearty and extravagant things, start to back away as others come in. Soon you will find yourself pushed to the outer rim of the guests. Back toward the door and leave. It all takes 20 minutes. You still have plenty of time to get home for *Animal House*.

29

Envy no one—ever

30

Believe everyone— always

∽

I realize that this rule seems to contradict the spirit of so many others. But when one gets down to it, life's basic choice is either to live cynically or innocently. I would choose innocence. I believe practically everything I am told, all the time. And, as a result, I am a ripe target for every chicanery, deception, and betrayal. I would hate to count how many times I have paid for trusting too many too much. And still, I think it preferable to trusting too few too little.

Believe everyone, and you will operate under the delightfully illusory opinion that life is well-intended. That in itself will make you feel young. Every worthy artist I know is an innocent, and the attitude allows him or her to create the world anew every morning. I begin each dawn feeling certain that the day ahead will be as fluent and open as the sea. Once in a while I am right. That's enough; a lot, actually.

~

31

Do not attempt to improve anyone, especially when you know it will help

∼⌐∽

The following situation will present itself to you over and over: There is a friend, a relative, an employee, an employer, a colleague, whose behavior flaws are so evident to everyone but themselves, you just know that a straightforward, no-punches-pulled conversation with them will show them the errors of their ways. They will in turn see the light at once and be forever grateful that only as good and caring a person as yourself would be so kind and so brave as to confront them.

Better still: From the moment you inform them about their bad table manners, their poor choices in clothing, their loudness, their deafness, their paranoia, they will reform on the spot. Their lives will be redeemed, and they will owe their renewed selves and all future happiness to you—honest, frank, and open you.

I implore you: When the muse of improvement whispers in your ear, swat it. I refer to rule 2. Nobody is thinking about you—unless you tell them about their faults. Then you may be sure that they are thinking about you. They are thinking of killing you.

～

32

If they tell you that
it's a long shot—it is

33

Never bring news of slander to a friend

~~~~~

It takes your enemy and your friend, working to-gether, to hurt you to the heart; the one to slander you and the other to get the news to you." The author is Mark Twain, and, of course, he is right. Still, this rule is very hard to accept because it tears at friendship in opposing directions. You want your friend to know if a slander has been brought against him, but you don't want to see him in pain, and you certainly do not wish to be the agent of his pain. You will tell yourself it is better that news of a calumny comes from you rather than from someone with malice in his heart. Yet, this is not so. If an ill-wisher tells someone that he has been slandered, the slanderee will automatically inure himself against the news to deprive the messenger of the pleasure of delivering the message. But if the news comes from someone he loves, his guard is down, and he is vulnerable.

The truth is—the world of little minds being what it is—that your friend will learn of the slander soon enough. And, if he is smart, he will raise the matter with you first, to ease your discomfort. By allowing him to do this, you will have placed the power of the situation in his hands, and much of the injury will have been diminished. The rest may be taken care of when the two of you agree to destroy the prick as soon as you get the chance.

34

It's not about you

In the late 1970s I was writing columns and editorials for the *Washington Post*. Because I knew nothing about any particular subject, it fell to me to write the paper's editorial whenever a prominent person died. So frequently did I write such pieces, that I soon became known by my colleagues as "Mr. Death"—not the most cheerful nickname, but at least it indicated a minor skill.

When Golda Meir passed away, Mr. Death was called upon to write an homage to her life and accomplishments. Rather than recite known facts, I wanted to get at least one quotation from someone who had known her personally. I was referred to a very powerful columnist of the time, whom I phoned with my request. "Could you tell me something especially revealing about Mrs. Meir," I asked him. "Oh, yes!" he said at once. "We were very close, you know. I shall never forget the day she leaned forward and told me: 'You are, without question, the best columnist in America.'"

It was fascinating to realize that this man—accomplished, admired, intelligent, worldly-wise—had not the slightest idea of how ridiculous he sounded. (I did not use the quote.) But what came off as merely a silly thing to say probably concealed a worldview; this fellow actually believed that all questions were about *him*. Trust Mr. Death: It's not about you—particularly when the "it" has to do with somebody's demise.

A few years ago, I went to a memorial service for a revered book editor and a very good guy. One by one, authors with whom this editor had worked came up to the pulpit in the church to speak of the deceased's mind and character. One eulogy went: "'John,' he once said to me, his eyes moist with tears, 'you are the best writer since Hemingway!'" Another: "'Mary,' he said, trembling from head to foot with joy, 'you are the best writer since Virginia Woolf!'" And so on.

I recall another memorial service where a man talked for nearly a half hour, recounting various tales of how much the dearly departed had relied on his excellent judgment.

It's not about you is a simple rule to follow if you concentrate on the question or the occasion at hand and ask yourself: What is required here? Though you are certain that you are the center of the universe, you might acknowledge, in one or two instances, that you ought to travel to another planet. Modern journalism has not been of much help in supporting this rule, which may be why it seems archaic. These days it is the way of journalism to assume that the story is only about the journalist—a media version of provincialism. It is normal today to read a newspaper story about a political assassination that begins: "I was feeling queasy that morning when news of the king's death reached me. Maybe it was the coffee."

Frank O'Connor, the great Irish short-story writer, used to speak of his relationship with Yeats, in part to elevate himself by association. It was all good-natured, if transparent. Before Yeats died, O'Connor would recall that "Yeats said to me . . ." After the poet's death,

O'Connor turned the recollections around: "I said to Yeats." I studied briefly with O'Connor in Dublin. And I shall never forget the day he told me: "Roger, you are the best writer since me and Yeats!" I miss him very much.

⁓

35

Never say any
of the following

⌐∾⌐

a. *"That's the best thing you've ever done!"* People assume that there is a consistency of perfection in their work, or, as a hidden thought, they assume that you assume so. If you tell them that something represents "the best thing you've ever done," they will hear: "How much better it is than all the other things you've done!" An absolute compliment will be interpreted as a comparative insult. You might try, alternatively: "That's the best thing *anyone* has done! Ever!" That should do it.

b. *"How much is this boat?"*

c. *"My door is always open."* Not only is this offer idiotic on the face of it; your subordinates (to whom such nonsense is addressed) will subvert it anyway. Your door will always be open until someone, usually a creep, walks through it, asks to "see you privately," and shuts it behind him or her. Then you may be certain that you are in for something stupid, malicious, and/or wholly in the interests of the one who has taken advantage of your open-door policy.

On the other hand, if you announce to your office "My door is always closed," people will grouse about you (which they will do no matter what position your door is in), but they may behave a little better, and, in any case, you'll get your work done.

In general, don't say anything you don't mean, and if you do mean it, don't say it anyway.

d. *"You look lovely today."* See a. Remember: Everyone looks lovely *every* day.

e. *"Why not?!"* or *"Oh, what the hell!"* or *"What have I got to lose?"*

f. *"Do we really need a contract?"*

~⌒

36

If you want to keep a man
honest, never call him a liar

~~~~

There is nothing funny about this rule, but I like it
anyway. It isn't mine: I heard it uttered by Clark
Gable in a movie, who attributed it to the Chinese. It
was said in the context of the wandering eye. Gable had
been lovingly faithful to his wife (Myrna Loy) until she
became suspicious that he was fooling around with his
secretary (Jean Harlow), which he was not. Only when
he was accused of infidelity did Gable begin to think of
the possibilities. Eventually everything turned out fine,
but the rule remains useful.

The deep wisdom in it is that we have a great
many people in us—good, bad, smart, stupid, faithful,

unfaithful—all the time. Given certain encouragements, some surface and some stay submerged. If you want to keep the more troublemaking people submerged, don't let the better people in you know that they exist. Quality does not always rise to the top.

〜

37

The waitress is not
waiting for you

$\sim\!\!\!\!\!\!\!\!\!\!\!\!\!\!\!\sim$

O ur touching, romantic natures are frequently
gripped by the notion that, though our current
lives are drab and deadened, a life of adventure and per-
petual excitement is just around the corner. For men
this vision often takes the form of waitresses. A man will
be sitting in a coffee shop, sipping his coffee, and
chomping on a wedge of unidentifiable pie that he has
ordered expressly because it was unidentifiable (that is
how men are). A comely waitress has brought him his
food. She walks away. He looks up. Suddenly, it comes
clear to him: All his life he has been seeking that waitress. He hears someone call her Pam. All his life he has
been seeking Pam. Tonight he will ask her out to dinner

and a movie. Tomorrow they will drive to South Carolina to be married. The day after tomorrow, he will be sick of his drab and deadened life with Pam, and, fortunately, he will find himself in a coffee shop where he is served by Chrissie.

Much time may be saved if he realizes that while he has been waiting for Pam, Pam has not been waiting for him. She has a drab and deadened life of her own, thanks to her husband, Lou, who, after a yearlong affair with Chrissie, is about to drop her for Janice, a waitress downtown. Pam has eyes for Marty, an insurance executive, who has a drab and deadened life with Darlene. Chrissie, tired of men, hankers for Janice. Are you following this?

38

Push the wheel forward

~~~

So many of the rules have been prohibitive or cautionary that I hesitate to offer this one. But since the point of this rule is to avoid hesitation, here goes.

The idea of pushing the wheel forward comes from a film I saw as a kid about test pilots in Britain attempting to break the sound barrier. The quite uncolorful title of the film was *Breaking the Sound Barrier*; and though it was technically fiction, it had the look and feel of a documentary. The plot was straightforward. Again and again, pilots would go up in their jets, increasing the speed until they hit that invisible wall of sound. When they did hit the wall, the planes started to shake terribly. The pilots would announce to the tower: "Buffeting,

buffeting!" Then they would pull back on the wheel in an effort to slow the plane down and stop the shaking. When that happened, the plane would go into a nosedive and crash to the ground. This happened repeatedly with every test.

Then one day a pilot went up and changed the pattern. When his plane hit the wall and began "buffeting," he did not pull back on the wheel. Instead, he pushed the wheel forward and immediately flew through the wall and broke the sound barrier.

I saw that scene when I was a little boy, and I can still feel the exhilaration of it today. The lesson was clear to me as a kid, and it should be clear for adults as well. Life gets very dangerous if you play it defensively or fearfully. Michael Jordan said that he rarely got injured because he never played at half speed. Life is only rewarding if you play at full speed. It is not only more fun, it is also safer.

This rule may seem aimed at the young, I know, but it will help one grow older. And the older you are, the more it will mean. It applies to everything—to love, business, finance, art, the help of others. When you reach critical speed, you fear that you're going too fast—

you've never traveled at such a speed—and everything in your system tells you to back off or back down. And here is where you must defy everything in your system. Say it, do it, make it, risk it. Your whole body is buffeting. You are miles above the earth. Push the wheel forward. There.

39

Dress for duress

～⌒～

Hedda Hopper was known for wearing flamboyant hats; Marianne Moore, for wearing tricorners; Mark Twain (and now Tom Wolfe) was known for wearing white suits; Arthur Schlesinger Jr. always wears bow ties. Each of these people is distinguished for more important things than clothing, but they deliberately chose outfits that would draw singular attention to themselves. They did so—it is commonly believed—to establish a sort of visual identity, a sartorial signature, that would affirm their celebrity.

But I think that there was another, more important reason—self-preservation. People who are notable for a particular manner of dress are protected in hard times because their signature outfits represent a lifetime, an entire biography. Here's the syllogism: The tricorner hat is Marianne Moore; Moore is a major modern poet; the tricorner hat means that you are looking at a major modern poet. When Moore wrote a very bad poem, one was still reminded by the hat that she was a very good poet. The outfit was a protection against bad times, bad moods, bad anything.

This, I believe, is why kings and queens wear crowns; why Superman wears his supersuit; why anybody in a prominent position finds an identifying outfit that says, all by itself: "Here is who I am, no matter what's going on right now." But making use of the rule does not require prominence. I know a perfectly regular guy who wears turtlenecks as his signature and a woman who dresses only in black.

Choose an item of clothing for which you will be immediately recognized. Wear it all the time. Any momentary bad spell will disappear quickly. Having a signature outfit removes you from reality; you become like a character in a play. And, as long as you are generally successful, there is the presumption of success about you. I wear a navy blue crew neck sweater on television most of the time so that people might notice the sweater and not the fact that I am sounding like an idiot. Knights wore suits of armor. You get the point.

40

A long and happy life
lasts five minutes

One would think that this rule would go without
stating, but many people actually believe that a
long life of uninterrupted happiness is a real possibility.
And they act on this belief! They change families,
careers, the structure of their faces, countries, everything, for no more substantial reason than they recall
five minutes of uninterrupted happiness in the past, and
now they wish to re-create the moment in perpetuity.
They even convince themselves that the five-minute
period they recall was really five years and giddily sub-
stitute the exception (bliss) for the rule (confusion,
doubt, misery, fear, confusion, and confusion). Happiness
is wonderful, but if you have had more than five consec-
utive minutes of it, it means that you weren't thinking.

41

Never work for anyone
more insecure than yourself

∿

There is a long list of people for whom one should never go to work—crooks, racists, liars—but the most dangerous of the lot are those who are in over their heads. Anyone who feels inadequate to a position of authority will inevitably: a) trust the wrong people for advice; b) betray you at the drop of a name; c) mess up the whole enterprise and throw everyone into unemployment. Such people may not mean to do any of those things, but they are driven, night and day, by a fear of exposure. They know that they are inept; you know that they are inept; they know that you know it. Better always to work for a competent tyrant. I am self-employed.

42

The unexamined life
lasts longer

~~~~⌒~~~~

People have been living for over a hundred post-
Freudian years with the idea that prolonged and
continuous introspection is good for one's mental
health, thus they fail to remember how miserable doing
this makes them. A certain amount of self-examination
is useful, but even that should be directed toward what
to do in a given situation and not at who you are.
However full your nights are with self-recrimination,
you are probably all right as a person (most people are).
How you ought to *act* when this or that occurs is another matter, and you might give that some self-inspecting
thought—two minutes, if you are being honest with

yourself—five, if you want to be dishonest first and then work your way around to the truth. Otherwise, aim your thoughts outward. Go for a run. Make a vase. Read a book. Yes, read a book where you may examine someone else's miserable life. Enjoy.

⌒ↄ

43

No, they don't—and so what?

This rule applies to a special circumstance. It is
meant for you people who are at least 50 years old,
and who used to work for people older than yourselves.
Now you work for people younger—much younger—
than yourselves. These young bosses do not remember
how good you are at what you do—that you have a long
history of being good at what you do. It is not your
fault that you have grown old. It is not their fault that
they haven't.

But you are offended by this state of affairs. You
expect your young bosses to automatically accord you
the respect which you deserve. And you do deserve it.
When they do not give it to you—when they spell out
exactly what it is they want in an assignment or feel that

they must explain things to you that you understood before they were born—you feel a painful affront. Don't they realize how very special you are, how gifted, how distinguished? Don't they understand that you ought to be treated like a work of art, an old master hanging on the wall?

No, they don't—and so what? The fact that there is no automatic recognition of your worth is good for you—rough on your ego, but good for your work. It may shake you up usefully, produce better results. It may even remind you why you like doing your work in the first place. And worry not. Soon all these young whizzes will be working for people much younger than themselves who will accord them no automatic appreciation either. Now, don't you feel better?

⌒

44

Abjure fame
but avoid obscurity

E nough has been written about the perils and penal-
ties of pursuing fame. Apart from the wealth of
neuroses it engenders and the sense of blinding unreal-
ity with which it obscures every endeavor, fame is hard
work. It is also remarkably unrewarding, especially in
our time when fame and importance are usually antipo-
dal. One has to decide whether the ability to get a last-
minute table in an overheated, overpriced restaurant or
a front row seat at a bad ball game is worth all the effort.
One also has to diet and look lovely all the time. One
has to smile at strangers.

On the other and more modest hand, the avoid-
ance of obscurity is a very good standard for life,

because it puts the emphasis on the quality of work. If, instead of seeking fame, you are more interested in simply meriting the approval of peers, the chances are better that you will accomplish this by drawing attention to the things you do rather than to some shimmering persona that you have manufactured for public inspection.

Meg Greenfield, the longtime columnist for *Newsweek* and editorial page editor for the *Washington Post*, who died in 1999 after a tough and dignified fight with cancer, could have had fame without half trying. Second to Kathrine Graham, Meg was the most powerful woman in Washington. But she actively cultivated a life from which the siren fame was barred. Instead, she chose to do good work steadily (see rule 45) and so was noticed and appreciated, and sucked-up to, and probably a little feared. Yet she never had to stretch herself into caricature to live up to a purposeless celebrity.

Her healthy attitude allowed her to maintain the best sense of humor in town. When I was doing editorials for the *Post*, I was given the assignment of writing about a Maryland man who had been arrested for murdering a goose on a golf course because the bird had gotten in his way. Having formed my ridiculous opinion as to how this case should be disposed, I asked Meg what title I ought to give the editorial. Without looking up from her desk, she said: "Honk If You Think He's Guilty."

Lewis Thomas, the biologist-physician-philosopher who wrote *The Lives of a Cell* and *The Medusa and the Snail*, was a similar type. He, too, died of cancer, of lymphoma. I knew Lewis for many years, and when he was ill, I asked him if I might write a piece about him. I told him that he had helped so many people understand the nature of living, that it would be valuable if he could also tell them something about dying. He agreed. Over the course of two years we talked together, during which he mainly avoided our subject. Finally he told me that after giving it some thought, he decided that it was more important to know how to live than how to die, and he said that the best criterion for a life was to determine whether it has been of use to others. If it were useful, it would be noticed.

Lewis died in November of 1993— about 10 days after my piece on him appeared in the *New York Times* magazine. During those 10 days, the magazine and I received hundreds of letters from Lewis's readers over the years who wanted to thank him for the learning and the wisdom his writing had given them. I read him some of the letters. When, in the last days, he fell into a coma, I continued to read him the letters; you never know. Not for a moment could Lewis have doubted that his life had been noticed.

45

Fast and steady
wins the race

～⌢～

Whatever it is that you do well later in life you
probably did exceptionally well at the beginning,
causing people to sit up and remark on how especially
gifted and capable you were. Now that you have done
your work for many years, you remember those times of
initial praise with a mournful melancholy. You would
like to cause that stir again. You won't. Don't worry. If,
indeed, you start to seek attention for what you do, you
are bound to do something so unlike you that others
may forget the work with which you have been quietly
but happily associated. Steady excellence is one of the
hardest things for Americans to recognize because it is

the antithesis of newness, revolution, and excitement. Yet those who achieve steady excellence lead contented lives, which are in fact a lot more appreciated than they may know. Excitement is a reasonable standard only for the young, who know what to do with it.

⌁

46

To thine own self be true— unless you would like to be someone else

~~◦

However excellent you are at what you do, you still may wish to be someone else. Go ahead. Authenticity is prized in our culture only insofar as how attractive the authentic being is. If you really don't like who you are, you may be right.

47

Culture rules

a. See no movie that has been called "exquisite."

b. Read no novel that has been called "brave."

c. Attend no concert that has been called "long, but worth every minute."

d. Attend no opera that begins with the word "*Der*."

e. Attend no other opera.

48

If it's just a teeny-weeny
bit wrong—destroy it

Advocates of word processors tend to promote the machines by pointing out how easy it is to make corrections. In the flick of a key one may transpose paragraph 19 for paragraph 37; chapter 5 may become chapter 20; and so forth. People tout these "conveniences" to illustrate the facility with which a manuscript may be repaired and how much time can be saved.

Nonsense. Time has actually been lost. In writing, if one thing is wrong, the whole thing is wrong. And the smaller the wrong thing appears, the larger the overall error. Writers spend months wondering what to do with the third sentence from the bottom of paragraph four, page 307, when they would be better off gently picking up the entire manuscript and walking ceremoniously to the trash can.

What is true for writing is true for other things. If an outfit is a little wrong, it is all wrong. If a friendship is a little wrong, it is all wrong. Think of little errors not as aberrations but as cautionary symbols, representative of the whole.

I realize that this rule will deprive you of the pleasure of pretending that a few minimalist repairs are all that your life requires. That, of course, is the purpose of these rules—to take away your fun.

49

Never think on vacation

~~~~~

S omething odd happens to the mind when it is on holiday; it begins to think that a holiday is its desired condition. And so, while the rest of the body is sunning, slaloming, spelunking, gazing stupefiedly out over the inexpressibly lovely sand dunes of Cape Cod or the glorious peaks of the Grand Tetons—that suddenly mirage into building sites—the mind begins to contemplate an entire future made up of revolutionary happiness. It asks itself: Why have you wasted your life up to this moment of clarity? This, *this* is who you were meant to be all along. "This" is usually followed by: A novelist, a sculptor, a painter of watercolors; a small but self-sustaining farmer, a vineyard owner, possibly a carpenter (though that takes training). Soon you are listening to your mind compose one long explanatory letter to your boss.

If it were possible to park one's mind at the gate of a resort or wherever one goes on vacation—the way cowboys were made to park their six-guns at the gates of Dodge City—holidays would never be lethally dangerous. Since that is not possible, do the next best thing: Don't think. Keep the mind in its safe and stupid mode, the way you like it when on vacation. Aren't these peaches the *best*?

50

[As long as I am on the subject] Change no more than one-eighth of your life at a time

~~~~~

The trouble with most people is that when they do decide to change their lives, they tend to think of changing everything all at once. Even if this were possible—it isn't—it would lead to disaster. When you are certain that it is time to become that novelist, sculptor, or watercolorist, change your shoes. See how the new pair fits. Then you might change the side of your head that your hair is parted on. How do you look now, big boy? That's plenty for the moment. In a few years, change your glasses.

51

Expect gratitude from everybody for everything

❧

Just kidding, of course. Expect gratitude from nobody for anything. It's not that you don't deserve gratitude or that, in a just world, you would not receive it. But this is planet Earth. And here, if you expect people to demonstrate gratitude for something you have done for them, you are in for a lot of steaming and fuming and wasted hours.

Once in a while, someone will actually show thanks for an act of kindness, sympathy, or generosity. But don't hold your breath; it is bad for your health. Keep an even keel by having no expectations. Then, on that very rare occasion when someone does show gratitude, you won't have a heart attack. Heart attacks can kill you. (Don't thank me.)

52

Live in the past, but don't remember too much

⌒

One only has to explain this rule to people under fifty. The first part is, in a way, unnecessary. It is impossible to live in any tense but the past. The present moves too fast; the future is the future. In Thornton Wilder's *The Skin of Our Teeth*, the fortune-teller says, "I tell the future. Nothing easier. But who can tell you your past, eh? Nobody!" For myself, I increasingly find that the past is where I most want to be. You may feel the same way.

But don't remember too much. I don't think I need to say any more about that.

53

Never do it for the money

~~~

I mean it.

54

Remember the Amana

Did you hear the story of the man who ordered an Amana freezer from an appliance store? The store promised that the freezer would be delivered on a certain day between 1:00 and 4:00 P.M., and it wasn't. The man phoned the store and angrily demanded to know where the freezer was. Told that it definitely would be delivered on the following day between 8:00 and 11:00 A.M., he remarked to his wife, "They had better do it this time or else!" The store failed to deliver the freezer again, and the man was livid. He called the store manager and yelled into the phone. He called his lawyer. His wife told him that he was making too much of the matter, that the Amana would arrive eventually, and that she was getting annoyed with him. He told her to shut up and asked whose side was she on anyway. Then he called the store again, and this time he threatened to kill the store manager. The manager called his lawyer. The wife, realizing that she had married a maniac, called *her* lawyer. In the end, the transaction cost the man his wife, $250,000 in damages, and the house in which he had planned to put the freezer.

Moral: Remember the Amana. Every one of life's little mishaps can be kept in perspective if one focuses on one's original goal—in this case, to acquire an Amana freezer. I invented this story, by the way, in case you are thinking of looking it up.

55

If you are strange enough, they will come

⌒

A good idea is to cultivate at least one wholly unreasonable facet of your behavior and to force more reasonable people to accommodate themselves to you. I, for example, do not use a word processor—in part, for some sound reasons (see rule 48) and, in part, for no reason at all. I do my writing on a yellow legal notepad and then on an electric typewriter, for which I have cornered the market on typewriter ribbons. Of course, there is no market for these other than myself and, perhaps, a dozen other oddballs. And I know that I really should start using a word processor and stop making life a chore for those who are cursed with handling my work.

Why do I persist? Not to be quaint. Not to be difficult, though I realize that I am. I cultivate this wholly unreasonable facet of behavior because I want things my way and because I know that, sooner or later, if I do not budge, people will bend their lives to mine. If I am strange enough, they will come. Editors never question why they must put my materials into the system for me. They have simply found it expedient to adapt to my strangeness, mainly because I have never indicated that I would adapt to them.

One ought not to carry such behavior too far or others will grow restive and you'll be cooked. And I do not advocate developing an eccentricity simply to amuse oneself or for the sake of tormenting others. But if you like doing something your way—no matter how odd that way might be—the world will heel.

The candy emperor, Forrest Mars, was the creator of M&Ms, and he insisted that the M on every M&M be printed in the exact center of each piece of candy. Often he would phone a sales associate in the middle of the night if he found that an M was not where it should have been, and he would order the candy to be recalled. Employees bristled. Mars died in 1999. Go out and get an M&M. Notice where the M is.

56

Never light the fire
from the top

∼∽

This rule refers to the value of process, to taking the time to do things right. Few people seem to understand this these days when so many processes can be circumvented—such as the quick acquisition of riches, the instant marriage of total strangers on a TV show, and the microwaving of dinners. Given all that, not for a moment do I imagine that this rule will be taken seriously. And if you do feel that a fire may be lit from the top, by all means try it.

57

The game is played
away from the ball

⌒⌒

I used to teach this idea to journalism students to make the point that the more interesting things in the news occur without making a big noise. The rule derives from something said by Eddie Sutton, now coach of the Oklahoma State University basketball team. When Sutton was coaching Arkansas, he asked his players what they did during practice. They answered, "Dribble and shoot." Then he asked them how much time they thought that they dribbled and shot during a 40-minute game—how many total minutes they had their hands on the ball. The players guessed 12, 14, 15 minutes. Sutton told them that a more likely number was 2 to 3 minutes, and he also told them what that meant in terms of the nature of the game of basketball. "Most of the game is played away from the ball," he said, meaning defense and getting into position for a pass.

In journalism, it is useful to look away from the ball because most journalists don't. They turn their heads toward a particular eruptive event and miss the continuous story, which may give a far more truthful picture. In wider contexts, people tend to do the same thing and thus, make judgments based on things that happen suddenly and explosively rather than on things that happen all the time.

Here's where this rule for aging comes in: The game is also played away from the ball when it comes to people. Do not judge others by their dramatic moments—how they may panic or become nasty or wild in a crisis—in contrast to their much different normal behavior. The people they are in repose are the people they are. The people they become in a crisis are the people they become in a crisis. If you like them better in a crisis, you might create a series of shocking events for them to respond to. But if you prefer them in the quieter moments, judge them away from the ball. Naturally, this applies to the way you would like them to look at you, too.

58

Apologize,
reconcile, give help

I told you these rules were easy.

Acknowledgments

∽

This book began with one column that I wrote in *Modern Maturity*, the magazine with the worst title in the world, but also with some of the best people for a writer to work with. One of them, editor Karen Reyes, suggested to me that the column might be expanded into a book (see rule 25). My thanks to her for wishful thinking and for ten years of happy and successful collaboration. During that blissful time, by the way, Karen and I never met, and we still haven't. There's a rule here somewhere.

I am grateful to my wife, Ginny, who sat through many fascinating breakfasts with her husband blurting out such conversation starters as: "How about this one?" or "How about *this* one?" I am grateful to our children by biology and marriage, Carl, Amy, John, Wendy, and Harris, for their existence and for keeping their noses out of my work.

My thanks as well to Harcourt's Jane Isay, chief of editors, for giving the manuscript more attentive intelligence than it deserved. And to Ronald Berman, former chairman of the National Endowment for the Humanities, who attempted to give the book some erudition, but failed. And to Amy Cacciola, my over-talented research assistant, who will dump me when her first novel is published. And to the delightful, though finicky, Midge McCagney, who made the manuscript presentable. And to my beloved, long-suffering agent, Gloria Loomis, who stoically accepts whatever nonsense I turn out.

I told Gloria that Jane Isay was the only editor I wanted to look at the book, and that if Jane didn't want the thing, to toss it. Those displeased by Jane's decision may wish to thank her directly.

Roger Rosenblatt